Cupcake Day

Cupcake Day

Poems by Alissa Sammarco

Turning Point

Published by Turning Point
P.O. Box 541106
Cincinnati, OH 45254-1106

ISBN: 9781625494740

Poetry Editor: Kevin Walzer
Business Editor: Lori Jareo

Visit us on the web at www.turningpointbooks.com

Cover Art: Wendy Cartwright, "Brighter Days," 2024
Author Photograph: Troi Gray

Dedicated to my mother and best friend, Melissa Sammarco, who taught me how to laugh more than cry. She taught me that art is life and not just the reflection that you wish you looked like.

Many thanks to the people in my life who inspired the love that went into these poems. Thanks to my husband who lived this work with me and proofread many versions. Thanks always to my father and mother who taught me how to care, especially when life was most difficult.

"The Architecture of Oncology" first appeared in *Black Moon Magazine*, Issue 9, January 2023.
"This is Becoming a Habit" first appeared in *Sheila-Na-Gig,* Volume 7.3, Spring 2022.

Contents

Rain

Rain,
great gusts
of sweat and torment fall
all around me while you swim
away

in channels
fraught with treacherous
currents that flow past eddies
where pictures of you, me – us –
dissolve.

The Architecture of Oncology

Ghosts walk back and forth
reflected in the waiting room windows
like ruby slippers dancing over yellow bricks
while we sit in chairs built sturdy

for those who are no longer
        sturdy.

Downstairs, radiation leaks
through cracks in my heart,
blurring lines between memories,
like sun through clapboards into dusty dark,

carefree as hair blowing in Caribbean breezes,
and I-love-you's scratched into a frosted cocktail bar
and dirty martinis with extra olives.
Leaks like wind between autumn and winter,

while butchers carve the living from the dead,
and shadows of lovers from loved ones.
Holding hands, holding elbows,
they shuffle along a highway

of pure gold-leaf uranium cobblestones
        chanting,

There's no place like home.
There's no place like home.

When a Stranger Asks in the Waiting Room

"Are you ok?"
Was it the sigh or the tapping
of my feet on the linoleum?
The room gets smaller every time I'm here.
At first, I sat looking down from the balcony,
watching people float reflections in
the floor to ceiling windows
surrounded by sun and grass and trees.
Everything was so bright.

They downgraded my seat from the balcony
to a room with people lined up behind masks.
Now, to this windowless room where the walls are close,
there are only four chairs here and the dark tv
hangs on the wall by the closet.
I jump as the elevator turns on,
gears and engines behind the wall, without warning.

This is not a waiting room.
This is an end,
a place to say goodbye
and hello again when we fall out the bottom
of a spiral wishing well where children roll pennies.
They spin around and around.
The closer they get, the faster they spin,
finally spit out into a golden spittoon.

The radiation is painless.
They told me it's painless.
But it hurts when I fall.
Is that why I sighed
and the man in the chair asked me,
"Are you alright?"

Dosage

You asked the radiology tech,
"Do you increase the dosage with each treatment?"
She said, "No, it's like antibiotics."
She said, "You can't take five doses at once,
but you can take one for five days."

But it's not at all like that.
If you took all the pills at once,
it wouldn't hurt.
But if you took all the radiation at once,
there would be nothing worth saving.

It's more like sunbathing,
falling asleep in the afternoon
until your skin turns red, blisters,
and peels off your shoulders.
No, it's more like a roast
you left in at one-thousand degrees.

But if you roast it slow,
it will be moist, cured in its own juice.
The tender bits separate from gristle,
and even though you are never the same,
you can pick the poison from the carcass
and savor what's left with a fine glass of Chianti.

Melting

When did summer wear out his welcome?
Through Christmas, he dropped lightning bolts
and watched the oaks finally shed their leaves.
He watched as deer rutted and pulled up saplings
looking for true love.

Yesterday, shoes by the door, I stepped outside,
two, no three steps to the newspaper
when winter cut my tip toe run.
Oh, how you deceived me
with daffodils and December roses,
that you would stay just a little longer.

The Crossing

Father crossed the threshold.
His eyes were starlight,
sparkling as he unveiled
a drawstring purse made of gilded leather
and marked with hieroglyphs,
Ra and Isis crossing the River Styx,
holding hands as they pass
between monuments that serve only men.

Coins clinked as they fell,
calling the faithful home.
Ra and Isis casting long shadows
over pyramid and sphinx.

He placed the purse in my hand,
chanting incantations as his fingers
traced the hieroglyphs,
passing on the magic of all that is buried
and drawing a map of where not to dig.

Words Like Raindrops

Are you ever
afraid that we
will evaporate
the way rainwater
tears on rosebuds?

They are perfect mirrors
between pink folds
that open as the sun
pushes its way
through storm clouds.

The droplets cry
only for a moment,
not even a kiss goodbye
to cool the tongues
that rhyme words wrapped
around each other
in perfect folds.

Lying Next to You

Each breath pushes us together
then fills sails to dreams
where I reach out
and fingers touch electric air
filled with salt and cumulus,
breaking trust and breaking ground.
The water licks the hull of my skiff
like tongues licking sun dried lips.
I lie in the bottom and watch the sky,
unsure who drifts faster, the clouds or I.
Dreams of islands where we once played,
where my children stayed,
running in and out of screen doors,
slapping hands on balls
rolling down halls.
Until the storm bursts,
raining down on this open skiff
tethered in safe harbor next to you.

This Is Becoming a Habit

You going to bed,
leaving me to linger
in front of the tv,
ice clinking as it rolls
in amber bourbon.
If I dare to get up,
if I dare ask you a question,
you answer like seashells
in the breeze
hung from driftwood
I found on the beach.
The steady rustling
of waves turning them,
cutting perfect holes
in the spires
of moonshells and oysters,
tritons and cowries.
Their voices answer nothing
like the wind chimes I made
from driftwood and fishing line
now hung at the bedroom door.

Two Years of Silence

Can't you please be quiet
or loud or something that I can
feel between fingers,
between toes, between the seams
of my clothes, holding us together
until they unravel
like sand sifts
on windy beaches, blows
away over the great expanse
of the sea, which harbors time
in seashells that whisper in my
ear.

You were right here with me
for two years, pecking and scratching
in my garden, looking for grubs
and finding cracked corn
I spread across the dirt.
You were steady in your
early morning crowing, 8 o'clock
sharp, rising to make coffee,
taking my hand and walking
through the gates I'd locked.

Stand next to me or in front or behind,
your shadow always touching mine
and even when you were far enough away
that I could no longer reach you
and smell the perfume of companionship.

Oh Hell, it couldn't have been two years
since you put a promise on my finger
and broke your vow never to do that
again.

Unmarked Graves

One day you will hold
all my insufficiencies against me.
They're buried on the hilltop,
names and dates chiseled
on tombstones,
worn away by weather.
One day, you will rub them
with charcoal and white paper
to remind me of all
I've tried to forget.
And then, maybe, together,
we can bury them in unmarked graves.

All I Really Ever Wanted

was for you to love me.
Maybe you were right when you said
I am the most selfish person
you ever knew.

Maybe it's true – I only wanted for me,
wanted, wanted, wanted,
selfishly,
to be loved.

Maybe you would stop loving me
when I grow old and no longer care for you.
Maybe all I ever wanted was
just to love you.

Sweet Basil

The basil stretches her neck high,
pregnant until blooms burst
and drop seeds the size of sand.
The basil won't wait for the night
to turn dew into frost
with its crystallized rainbows,
the embodiment of our last moments
before everything sleeps,
before we sleep,
drawing closed the curtains
against the loneliness of cold,
against the endlessness of lonely.
In the spring, if the squirrels
have not foraged them,
the sweet basil will return.
It's time to let her bolt.

There Is a Reason Why

they will die and return without end,
those tunes plucked by bare fingers against the sky
as soft flakes fall over leaves, over toes.
Damn the cold – Damn the cold!

There is a reason why the locust tree
was planted in the yard between me and the world.
Through the kitchen window, I watch her change
singing blue tones in October winds as autumn steps in.
It is marked by lichen-drawn spots, constant as the seasons.
Her leaves lie at her feet, cast down like naughty children.
Do they beg to be forgiven? Do they beg to be let back in?
Do they feel winter wrap tight, a cocoon for their chrysalis?

There is a reason why the window is over the sink.
I move the plants inside, and a squirrel waits in the window,
looking for the pots where he hid a hundred secrets
all summer long. Begging me to let him in.
But how could I give back what I have stolen?
Planting seeds in shallow graves over and over again.

Falling into the Barrel

you tread water, trying to sink
your fingers into the cracks
between boards, into knotholes,
waiting for the spigot to open.
If you're lucky, the drought
will dry you out
and you can stand tippy toe
until the next rain,
swimming only side to side
instead of for your life.

Extinct

Vines hung down
from ash trees
now extinct.
Barefoot trails
and blackberry stains
on fingers and face,
green mock-oranges
low on thorny branches.
Dogs barked,
then stopped,
then barked again.
Titmouse
or rabbit
or squirrel
scurried below.
Light faded
and night came
sudden,
big,
dark.

Cupcake Day

The doctor came in the room, *Congratulations!*

After a week of radiation, getting weaker each day,
After a week of feeling like nothing was happening
except the giant claw with its pointed fingers
shooting gamma rays until something inside boiled over.

Congratulations! He said,
You've completed your treatment.
We'll check to make sure

> *— you're cured*
>> *— 6 weeks*
— you'll be cured.

Where's my cupcake? I asked. He didn't have one.
You wanted to buy one with frosting and sprinkles.
But I said, *no, Cupcake Day is done,*
and 'cured' is a strange word to speak out loud.

Dip My Fingers into the Sky

Between cotton candy strings
twirled around my finger like a wedding ring.
Breasts pink and round,
firm silhouettes against stratus clouds
where crystalline tears
carry rainbows to far and future fields.

Hold me here
where I am everything.

And the Sky Went on Forever

An endless whitewashed picket fence
holds back the heavens,
broken in places, uneven
where the dogs can get through.
God doesn't worry who comes in and out.
He never locks the latch
or turns off the sun.
But sometimes, it is obscured
by the moon, by the earth,
or by a single picket
placed just right between us and Him.

Alissa Sammarco is a writer and attorney who lives in Cincinnati,
Ohio. She has lived all over the country and has spent her life being
captivated by the beauty of the American West and South, as well as
the woodlands of the Ohio River Valley. This beauty helps fuel the
vivid imagery in her work. She studied creative writing and economics
at the University of Rochester, and returns to poetry from her career
in law. Alissa's poetry has appeared in numerous print and online
journals including Sheila-Na-Gig, Black Moon Magazine, Evening
Street Review, Hags on Fire and more. She is the author of three
chapbooks: *Beyond the Dawn, I See Them Now,* and *Mon Landing Day*.
You can find more information and order books at
www.AlissaSammarco.com.

Made in the USA
Columbia, SC
06 January 2025

49336821R00019